THE MEASURE AND THE PLEDGE OF LOVE

For
Anne, Clare, Alec and Patrick

Peter F. Barrett

The Measure
and the Pledge
of Love

REFLECTIONS ON THE CROSS

THE COLUMBA PRESS / APCK

First published in 2002 by
The coluмвa press
55A Spruce Avenue, Stillorgan Industrial Park,
Blackrock, Co Dublin
and
APCK
St Ann's, Dawson Street, Dublin 2

Cover by Bill Bolger
Origination by The Columba Press
Printed in Ireland by ColourBooks Ltd, Dublin

ISBN 1 85607 389 0

Contents

Preface

The majority of the contents of this book were delivered as addresses for the traditional Good Friday Three Hours' Service, first in Saint George's Church, Belfast and more recently in Saint Mary's Cathedral, Limerick. They have been consolidated somewhat, but remain primarily reflections upon the crucified Lord Jesus preached within the context of the Liturgy of Good Friday. Collectively and individually, they seek to relate the mystery of the love of God in Christ, supremely focused in the crucifixion, to the devotional life of the pilgrim disciple. They are joined by other reflections which seek to link the awesome events of Good Friday to five major festivals of the church's liturgical cycle.

The title derives from a line in the last verse of a well known hymn, often sung at passiontide in the Church of Ireland, which begins 'We sing the praise of him who died' (written by the Irish hymn writer Thomas Kelly). The hymn encourages us to ponder the fact that behind the horror of it all, in which every age and all conditions are enfolded, there is an eternally loving purpose which both reveals and heals the best and worst of the human condition. By allowing the story to more fully embrace us, we open ourselves to the possibility of transformation. We discern that the cross reveals both the measure of the wonder of God's love in Christ for each of us and the measure of our capacity for selfishness and wickedness. But we discern too that it is God's eternal pledge of his abiding love for his creation, a love which is indeed flesh of our flesh and heartbeat of our heartbeat, drawing out of us the sting of sin for the sake of love and sacrificial service. We enter such mystery that such mystery may more fully enter us to the glory of God, to whom be the glory to the ages of ages.

The book is intended for individual or group study, and

would be of particular interest during Lent or Holy Week. Each chapter concludes with a prayer and some suggestions for further discussion / reflection.

I wish to express my gratitude to Seán O Boyle, The Columba Press, for his encouragement in producing this book, to Mr Edward Denniston, English-teacher at Newtown School, and to the Right Rev'd Michael Jackson, Bishop of Clogher, for their helpful comments on the text.

The scripture quotations contained herein are from *The New Revised Standard Version of the Bible*, Anglicised Edition, copyright 1989, 1995 by the Division of Christian Education of the National Council of the Churches of Christ in the United States of America, and are used by permission, all rights reserved.

All hymns are from *The Church Hymnal*, Fifth Edition, Oxford University Press 2000, unless otherwise stated.

Peter F. Barrett, Waterford
The Feast of the Transfiguration of our Lord, 2002

The God of the Cross

O Saviour of the world,
who by your cross and precious blood has redeemed us, save us
and help us, we humbly beseech you, O Lord.
(Traditional Prayer of the Liturgy of Good Friday)

Good Friday is a day of withdrawal and penitent reflection for the Christian. But it is supremely a day of profound thanksgiving. We deliberately withdraw from the rush of life (and sadly there is a great rush about, even on a Good Friday, for most on this island), to draw closer to the Lord Jesus and to him crucified. Almost, as it were, if this does not sound too blasphemous, to support him in his last hours of agony.

Of course, the great mystery is that Christ crucified needs no support; indeed, he supports us eternally by, with and through his ever blessed cross. But in a sense, time stands still as we seek to still ourselves to survey not just the wondrous cross, but our wondrous Lord on his throne of glory. For in spite of the horror of it all – the shouting of the crowd, the smell of sweat and blood, the noise of the hammer – there is, at its heart, a sense of glory about it all. Did not Jesus say: 'And I, when I am lifted up from the earth, will draw all people to myself.'(John 12:32) How true these words of our Saviour are for us, to us, and countless others in time and for eternity. Some words familiar to us as a passiontide blessing aid this first reflection on the God of the Cross:

> Christ draw you to himself and grant that you find in his cross a sure ground for faith, a firm support for hope and the assurance of sins forgiven.

How can the cross of Christ provide us with a sure ground for faith, a firm support for hope and the assurance of sins forgiven? I believe that it does, for it reveals in a unique and unrepeatable way the nature of the God whom we seek to worship and to serve. To concentrate on the cross alone would be idolatrous. The reason that we can find faith, hope and forgiveness lies in the terrible beauty of the One who hangs upon it: Jesus our Lord, sometimes described in the ancient Gaelic tradition as 'The High King of the Friday'.

If a non-Christian or a non-believer were to ask me 'What is your God really like?' I would not show them a beautiful part of the countryside and say I believe that he created this, true enough as I believe this to be. Neither would I point to the beauty of a complex equation or to a magnificent piece of art, and say that he inspired this, true enough as I believe this to be also. Rather, would I point to a 'green hill far away', outside the walls of that tragic yet wonderful city of Jerusalem, and try to relive in the mind's eye, somehow, someway, the scene of crucifixion we recall each and every Good Friday. For it is here at Calvary that I believe the true nature of God is revealed: in scenes of untold and unimaginable suffering and pain; indeed, even in death itself. God so loved the world that, in Christ, he loved it to the bitterest end. In Christ, God is God of the dead and the living, things seen and yet unseen, things which are yet to be as well as things which are. Archbishop Michael Ramsey has written:

God is Christlike, and in him is no unChristlikeness at all. (A. M. Ramsey, *God, Christ and the World*, p. 99).

Further, our blessed Lord does not die alone. He dies between two fellow sufferers, surrounded by the shouts of derision and worldly indifference to justice. He dies as he lived, in the midst of the pain of others, yet supported by the faithful few. It is all there on Calvary's hilly dump.

But the Christian understands such mystery solely in terms of love. For 'God is love' (1 John 4:8), and in Christ the Father's love in the fellowship of the Holy Spirit embraces the mystery of the totality of life, including death. The Christian trusts that such love is the creative, sustaining and re-creative beginning and end of existence, for life in Christ's love is eternal. Love holds all, sustains all. To borrow from Dante, it is 'the love that moves the sun and the other stars' (*Paradiso* 23:145). At Calvary, I place my deepest conviction in the assertion of Saint Paul that 'in Christ, God was reconciling the world to himself' (2 Corinthians 5:19) Indeed, the writer of the first epistle of John affirms: 'In this is love, not that we loved God but that he loved us and sent his Son to be the atoning sacrifice for our sins' (4: 10).

For each of us *Via crucis, via lucis*, the way of the cross is the way of light because it is the way of love. But for the Church that love is no abstract or philosophical concept. Rather from crib to cross we believe such divine love to have taken human life in Christ, and become flesh of our flesh and heartbeat of our heartbeat; the heartbeat of Christ in tune with our heartbeat so that we may echo the heartbeat of God and reflect the harmony of heaven in our relationships and society. In the life and death of Christ Jesus, God takes upon himself, takes deep into his heart of love, 'nature red in tooth and claw'.

The cross reveals the measure of such love, the length and depth as well as the height of the love of God. It does so not by standing in isolated and isolating suffering, but by being rooted and grounded within and amongst suffering, its arms reaching out to all who would be enfolded in such an embrace of love.

The cross, through the passion and death of its crucified Lord, visually expresses all that is left unsaid by its same Lord in his telling of the story of the Good Shepherd (John 10:11ff): how that God in Christ, like the Good Shepherd, goes the extra mile, climbs the highest height, enters the darkest depth to seek and to save the lost by, with and through love. Like a shepherd with his crook, so God in Christ uses the cross to reach down, to draw back, and to lift up the broken and the wandering. Truly his is a 'love that will not let me go'. There is nothing that you or I have or have not done, nothing you or I have experienced, no matter how distressing or how shameful, that is beyond the healing power of the God of the cross. Our past is transformed by the disfigured but ultimately transfiguring Lord Jesus, for 'by his stripes we are healed' (Isaiah 53: 5). Indeed, an early Church Father, Origen, took such an extravagant claim to its logical conclusion in asserting that Christ would forever be on his cross until the last wanderer returned into Christ's loving fold.

Here then is no sentimental picture of the God and Father of our Lord Jesus Christ, or of a God who is some kind of disinterested 'prime mover'. Neither I hope is this a romantic picture which reduces 'the Lord of glory' (1 Corinthians 2: 8) to a hero of some mythical tale. Rather, as Canon W. H. Vanstone emphasises (in the hymn found in his book *Love's Endeavour, Love's Expense*) the God and Father of our Lord Jesus Christ is no monarch, distant and removed. Rather, his 'aching, spent arms of love' sustain the world; his weakness gives us 'power to be'.

Here is a message for those today demanding signs and those seeking wisdom in the things of God. Those who desire the balm of God without the sacrifice of Christ; forgiveness without a spirit of repentance; new beginnings without a death to the past.

Of course, we can be brought close to God by things of beauty, truth and wonder. Those scenes, creations, moments which leave us breathless with delight and which bring us to our knees in awe, almost as it were in the one embrace. They can be on the 'Grand Canyon scale', or in moments of privacy and indeed intimacy. Such intimations of immortality or the 'oneness of all things', involve our humanity completely. We feel ourselves to be on holy ground: here and not here, present yet absent. We are fit only for one thing: worship. But the cross earths all and for better for worse, for richer for poorer, confronts us with the one truth that really matters; the one reality that is eternal because it truly sets us free, namely, the love of God not in any speculative sense but in the profoundly personal. '*Cor ad cor loquitur*,' 'heart speaks to heart', saying as it were, 'Christian, lovest thou me?'

I never fail to take inspiration from a particular incident between Jesus and Saint Peter recorded by Saint Luke. Jesus has just celebrated the Passover Meal with the disciples and, turning to Peter, he prophesies his denial and his restoration: 'Simon, Simon, behold Satan demanded to have you that he might sift you like wheat, but I have prayed for you that your faith may not fail; and when you have turned again, strengthen your brethren' (Luke 22:31-32).

The Greek word which we translate 'turn again', *metanoia*, can also be used for repentance. Our Lord once said that it was upon Peter's profession of faith that he would build his church; he didn't say upon the beloved disciple John, who was there at the foot of the cross but upon Peter who wasn't there because he had denied Jesus and had run away in tears. Even a rock can be shattered, but from the pieces there can emerge something new. After denial and betrayal there would be restoration and renewal. What is true of Peter is true for us.

Our life in Christ should consist not in dwelling over the inevitable consequences of our frailty and weakness, but upon the glorious invitation of our Lord to 'come to me, all you that are weary and are carrying heavy burdens, and I will give you rest' (Matthew 11: 28).

This is an ever-gracious encouragement, day and daily, to pick ourselves up, dust ourselves off, and start all over again. To start out afresh, as if for the first time in the ever-welcoming companionship of the Holy Spirit. No recrimination awaits us, only the welcome of a loving Father who wishes the best for our lives both now and for eternity.

Prayer
Help us, O Holy Spirit, to see in Christ and him crucified
both the measure of the love of the Father
and the measure of the weakness of our condition,
so that we may be lifted out of any complacency in faithfulness,
and renewed in trustfulness and service
by the power of such sacrifice;
for your glory and the sake of the kingdom
we pray this. Amen.

For consideration
How can the cross be described as an object of beauty?
How does the pain of the cross speak of the presence of God?
Why does the seed of our returning lie in our turning away?

The Politics of the Cross

'That same day Herod and Pilate became friends.'
(Luke 23:12)

The method of dating the passing of time according to the 'year of the Lord', *'Anno Domini'*, owes much to the events of this week which we call 'holy'. But why are they holy? What is holy about public crucifixion? What is wholesome about schemers and rabble rousers? What is holy about betrayal and denial? What is holy about blood, sweat and tears? Many of us are more than familiar with the description of something being suitable 'for adults only'. A programme, a film, a publication is, in short, 'X certificate'. Not even in the company of an adult is an under 18 permitted to see it.

We do well to consider that, in a way, Good Friday is for adults only for we are recalling the judicial murder of an innocent 33 year old man on charges based on little or no supporting evidence. In short, all is expediency. This is indeed heady stuff, demanding of us a strong stomach. What is ultimately involved is corruption in the highest, indeed the holiest of places. Worse, the means of carrying out the sentence of execution is one of the most cruel, most painful known to humankind and, believe it or not, it is carried out not in secret but at noon day in full public gaze at the eve of a festival weekend, the busiest time of year.

But the story line claims that we are somehow involved in such seediness. Involved because by and through these events a claim is made in time for all time: 'Is it nothing to you, all you who pass by? Look and see if there is any sorrow like my sorrow' (Lamentations l: 12). Why it should be

more than 'nothing' is a sub-text of the sum of our reflections. It is more than nothing because of the One who
makes it holy, who transforms this dreadful scene of
squalour by the stature of his presence, the quality of his
patient, enduring love. It is the Lord Jesus who transforms
this scene of human wickedness, weakness and degradation by his awesome silence and the inner strength of his
majestic stature. Because of this we call this Friday 'Good
Friday', and it is the Lord Jesus who turns this week of
darkness and intrigue into a truly Holy Week. But we cannot avoid its machinations; we must go through them for
we see before our eyes the fulfilment of Christ's prophecy
that, 'He must go to Jerusalem and undergo great suffering at the hands of the elders and chief priests and scribes,
and be killed, and on the third day be raised' (Matthew
16:21). In focusing upon the politics of the cross, we shall
try to place the crucifixion of our Lord in its contemporary
context by teasing out one or two factors which led to an
unholy alliance between, if you like, church and state.

The 'day' referred to by Luke in his account of the arrest
and trial of Jesus is a Friday, better known today as Good
Friday. Let's recall the scene: It's the early morning follow-
ing the night in which Jesus both instituted the eucharist
and was betrayed: the day of days in this week of weeks.
Jesus, having been arrested the previous evening at the
Garden of Gethsemane has been brought to the house of
Caiaphas, the High Priest at that time. To this day the place
is remembered for another act of human frailty, namely
Peter's denial, and a church now stands here with the un-
enviable title of St Peter in Galicantu, St Peter of the
Cockcrow.

But morning is breaking and in order to, as it were, get
rid of Jesus before the start of the Sabbath at sunset later
that day Caiaphas, after questioning him and finding him

guilty of the capital crime of blasphemy, sends Jesus to the Governor Pontius Pilate for judicial sentencing. However, Pilate has not the power to sentence Jesus to death for the crime of blasphemy. So, it is asserted that Jesus claimed to be a king, which is a political crime. In the Empire there can be no king but Caesar. The sentence for such a crime is death, and death not in the Jewish fashion by stoning but in the Roman mode by crucifixion.

But initially, Pilate is not so pliant and does not find him guilty. He is cautious when confronted by the flimsiest of evidence. Learning that Jesus is a Galilean he decides to send him to Herod to be tried under local law. Herod, Pilate's underling, his official Tetrarch, has come up to Jerusalem from his headquarters in Galilee to celebrate the Passover Festival. When Herod saw Jesus, we read, 'He was very glad, for he had been wanting to see him for a long time, because he had heard about him and was hoping to see him perform some signs' (Luke 23:8).

But we soon read that Herod 'questioned him at some length, but Jesus gave him no answer' (Luke 23:9). Instead, in the context of what may be described as a mock trial with the chief priests, scribes and soldiers looking on accusingly, Jesus, dressed we read in 'an elegant robe' (Luke 23:11), as if to heighten this sense of ridicule, was returned to the Governor by Herod. This action in itself is significant because it was not normal procedure for a Jew to hand over to the occupying power a fellow Jew to face the possibility of the death sentence. Luke does not interpret this in terms of a subordinate fulfilling a legal obligation. Rather, Luke sees it as a gesture of friendship on Herod's part towards Pilate: 'That same day Herod and Pilate became friends with each other; before this they had been enemies' (Luke 23:12).

Who was Herod? It's important to say that he was not

the Herod mentioned at the birth of Jesus. He is his son, Herod Antipas, the Herod who agreed to the beheading of John the Baptist, and we read that he was upset about having to fulfill his rash promise to the delectable Salome. Yet here, he is willingly handing over Jesus, a fellow Galilean, not like John to the whim of a personal mood, but to the full force of the Roman legal system against which there was no appeal for those who were not citizens of Rome (unlike Saint Paul later – see Acts 25:6-12). No doubt personal weakness or the desire for popularity with Pilate were at play here – psychological factors if you like. But it is important to try to discern a less obscure interpretation of Herod's motives. Other factors were involved in producing this sequence of events which are important for our understanding of the politics of the cross, the politics behind the death of Jesus.

A key lies with a question asked earlier of Jesus when before Caiaphas. Jesus had been directly asked the question, 'Are you, then, the Son of God?' (Luke 22:70). This damning question would be echoed some hours later when the crowd would shout, 'If you are the Son of God, come down from the cross' (Matthew 27:40).

Now to be the Son of God implied, within its layered meaning, Messiahship, and to be the Messiah was to be the long expected anointed king of Israel. This longing of the Jewish nation for God to step into history and liberate them from Roman oppression, just as Moses had freed them from slavery in Egypt, was an ever-present reality, particularly at every Passover. The mood at this Passover was equally expectant, and it is important not to underestimate this sense of expectancy at this time, for the God of Abraham, Isaac and Jacob was a God who acted in history through covenant with his chosen people, and there was a sense that the time was close at hand, was about to be fulfilled. For sure, this expectation was heightened by the entry of Jesus the previous Sunday to the cries of palm-waving crowds, symbolising their hope that truly God was about to fulfill his promise. But now, almost in retrospect as it were, we must once again pause and ponder the following:

What sort of Messiah is it who challenges by reinterpreting such expectation on his own terms, without reference to the scribes and pharisees who are, if you like, the guardians of the flame? Indeed, for nearly three years this rabbi from Galilee has been challenging such guardianship by disregarding their kosher laws and Sabbath observance, by keeping disreputable company, not just with drunkards and sinners but with tax collectors and the sick in body and mind. Jesus challenges the received wisdom, by living not only within but also without the pale of custom and due observance, on the borderlands of faithfulness if you like. Yet the expected Messiah was supposed to uphold and to vindicate the received tradition of the Torah, the Law, which clearly defined the covenant and which kept Israel pure as a nation. As scripture says, 'He came to what was his own, and his own people did not accept him' (John 1:11). For Herod, such behaviour demanded serious enquiry and explanation. Hence the three accusations recorded by Luke, which were used against Jesus when before Pilate for the first time: 'They began to accuse him, saying, we found this man perverting our nation, forbidding us to pay taxes to the emperor, and saying that he himself is the Messiah, a king' (Luke 23:2).

In short, Jesus is accused of leading the people astray, urging people not to pay taxes, claiming to be the Messiah. But Jesus had not led the people astray; rather, he had encouraged the people to see in his loving concern the true, humane face of the Torah, and in so doing illustrating the inclusiveness indeed the universality of the law and the prophets which he came 'not to abolish but to fulfill' (Matthew 5:17). He had encouraged the lawful payment of taxes (see Matthew 22:15-22). He constantly warned his disciples to keep his identity secret, not to proclaim his messiahship (see for example Matthew 16:20). What Herod and his party failed to recognise was that in Christ, God was redefining messiahship. But such a redefinition was of course too novel, too threatening both to the religious and the political status quo.

It is a truism to say that any mixture of politics and religion is potentially destructive. The history of this island bears this out to the present day. Theocracies of whatever hue have a tendency either to explode or to implode. Powerful institutions can seek power through exploitation of the legislature, shaping and reshaping laws into idols. Such imperialism masquerading as democracy enslaves the consciences of those it purports to represent and to serve. What is the duty of the individual or the minority for whom the way of the majority is not the way of liberating truth? Such is but one issue posed by the politics of the cross.

In entering Jerusalem with the support of the crowds, Jesus was almost giving the authorities one last chance to respond to the revitalised vision his message and ministry offered them for the renewal and reform of their, and ultimately his, people. But he threatened their peace and the peace of Jerusalem at its busiest time, a peace which the Roman authorities expected and required them to maintain, to the extent that their official positions, if not their lives, were under threat. In these and many other ways, Jesus antagonised the establishment and provided rich pickings not only for selective accusation but for united action against him when the hour was expedient. Only the politics of gesture, the feigned gesture of friendship on Herod's part towards Pilate, could secure the desired outcome, namely, the end of this radical Galilean and, with his death, the end of his potentailly subversive following and message. Here then is part of the explanation behind some of the machinations of these dark hours. But where does Rome fit in ? How does Pilate respond to Herod's gesture of friendship? We shall see when we explore the shame of the cross.

Prayer
Loving God in whom the true authority of love
and the real justice of peace abide,
guide by your Holy Spirit
all called to positions of leadership
in our community and land,
that being responsive to the needs
of those whom they seek to serve,
they may further the coming of your inclusive kingdom;
for the sake of Jesus Christ our Lord. Amen.

For consideration
Is expediency in public life desirable?
Can one be a 'christian politician'?
To what extent is the church counter-cultural in our
society today?

The Judgement of the Cross

'You would have no power over me
unless it had been given you from above.'
(John 19:11)

The American theologian, Reinhold Niebuhr, when addressing a group of students for the ministry, is reported as having said: 'Never preach a God without wrath who brought man without sin into a kingdom without judgement through the ministrations of a Christ without a cross.'

Strong words, and I'm sure that they were not easily forgotten by his students either. Yet they are words of relevance, not least when so much of our emphasis is, rightly, upon the love of God on Good Friday. It is out of love that God sent his only Son to die for us and for our salvation. It is in love that he shed his precious blood for us; it was for love that we are redeemed and restored.

Yet, this is no Jesus meek and mild. Neither is Jesus the divine victim, the subject of a brutal father; or as Shakespeare would have it in King Lear: 'As flies to wanton boys, are we to the gods; they kill us for their sport' (Act 4: scene 1). In spite of his apparent weakness, Christ Jesus was in control. Indeed, he was the one who united disparate groups against him in the first place. His hidden strength united their unrecognised weakness: 'You would have no power over me unless it had been given you from above.' The apparently helpless Jesus is certainly no pale Galilean. Rather, he rules through his silence, and controls by his very passivity. The thirst of the cross, the pain of the cross, the darkness of the cross, all judge us. If the cross is the divinely appointed means of our reconciliation in Christ, it is also the seat of judgement. The measure by which and through which our sins are not only carried, but are weighed, are removed, having first been borne.

If with Niebuhr we can in any way speak of the wrath of God, then it is in terms of the intensity of desire in God's love for us and for our salvation. For the love revealed at Calvary shows us that God will go to any length, even to the grave and gate of death, to expose and to overcome all that is not godly and wholesome, all that makes us worship at other altars, all that enslaves and restricts us, and makes us less than our best selves.

The gospel, by which we seek to live and to die, is a gospel of grace. But it is also a gospel of judgement causing us to cry out 'God, be merciful to me, a sinner' (Luke 18: 13). The judgement of God revealed in the cross shows not only how far God in Christ is prepared to go in order to come to our aid, but equally how far he has to go to bring us to our senses. If Christ had to die, and to die such an awful death, then something must be dreadfully wrong in the state of humanity. Well do we sing: 'A second Adam to the fight, and to the rescue came' (Hymn No 108).

The cross surely reveals to us the measure of the seriousness of our condition apart from the love of God in Christ. In short, it reveals the terrible cost of sin in our human condition, and not just its remedy. In the searing light of the utter holiness of God, sin has no place; in the searching gaze of the eyes of Christ, sin has no merit. Its propensity to tarnish, to corrupt and ultimately to destroy everything with which it comes into contact had to be confronted, had to be judged by the sacrifice of Christ, the Lamb of God.

Some words from a dearly beloved passiontide hymn prise slightly open for us a door into a deeper understanding of what is involved in such judgement:

There was no other good enough
to pay the price of sin ...
We may not know, we cannot tell
what pains he had to bear. (Hymn No 244)

As these words imply, a price had to be paid to meet the insatiable demands of scheming people. That price is placed before us on Good Friday as none other: that of the death of the Lord Jesus Christ. When we are speaking of the Lord's death, we are speaking of untold pain and agony, suffering and the cruelest of deaths, before which the very angels veil their faces. More, it is the death of an innocent, lovely, loving man for the very people who put him under such a sentence. The judgement of the cross reveals the weight of suffering that God is willing to endure out of love for his wayward creation. It also reveals the depths of our potential for cruelty and wickedness. As has been said, 'sin nailed him to the cross, but love held him there.'

We must never underestimate the weight of the agony, mental, physical, spiritual borne by the Lord for us and for our salvation, and for all creation. The weight of the agony is expressive of the weight of the sin of the world, yet all is borne in love. We must never underestimate the pain in spite of the lack of descriptive details used by the gospel writers. Indeed, the evangelists, the gospel writers, do not dwell on the process of crucifixion but merely refer to the fact: 'They crucified Jesus' (for example, Luke 23:33). But contemporaries would well have understood what those few words encapsulated, for crucifixion was a common sight throughout the regions of the Roman Empire. Crucifixions were regularly held at the same place in many areas as an overt means of quelling rebellion or sedition, as a frightening warning to high and low alike. However, if you find it hard to believe that sin literally 'nailed Jesus in the end', or if you find it equally hard to believe that love could so constrain a man to freely, willingly endure such a death, then pause for a moment and examine the background.

We read of several 'to-ings and fro-ings' with Jesus during the night and early morning following his arrest, from the High Priest's house to the Sanhedren's meeting place, eventually ending up with Pilate via Herod. All this took place so that Jesus could be trapped into a treasonable or blasphemous confession. Jesus was taken, if you like, from pillar to post. Then there was the search for witnesses, the agitation of the crowds, some of whom must surely have greeted Jesus earlier in the week with acclamation. We can only imagine the desperation and the scheming that was going on within and between the authorities. Their jealousy and fear were beyond control and were fusing into a deathly combination. Yet Pilate could say of the defenceless Jesus: 'I find no basis for an accusation against this man' (Luke 23:4). But soon we read: 'So Pilate gave his verdict that their demand should be granted' (Luke 23: 24).

Surely, surely, there is something wrong here? Actions and attitudes are so charged with emotion that reason, not alone justice, has disappeared. Yet of Jesus what do we read? Primarily of his silence, and amongst his few words these are writ large: 'Father, forgive them; for they do not know what they are doing' (Luke 23:34). Good Friday's cross judges sin, experiencing its gruesome sting, yet ultimately, it is love not condemnation which reigns from the tree: 'For God so loved the world that he gave his only Son, so that everyone who believes in him may not perish but have eternal life. Indeed, God did not send his Son into the world to condemn the world, but in order that the world might be saved through him' (John 3:16-17).

Divine judgement has a moral not a retributive flavour

to it. God in Christ seeks to reconcile not divide that which is apart, to seek and to save that which is lost. The judgement of God is a judgement made plain on the cross. It calls us to look here for grace to persevere and in so looking, to turn away from all that nailed the King of Glory to the tree. The tree of his ever blessed passion and death has power because on it Christ reverses the judgement cast on him by Pilate and the crowd, and by, with and through love, judges the world. In so doing he brings us to our knees in sorrow and in wonder. But in the same breath we are raised to a new stature in thanksgiving through the call to repentance and new beginnings.

Accountability is not a quality with which contemporary society is entirely comfortable. Progress often omits the recognition of the potentially positive fruits of failure, personal and communal. Judgement occurs only when we are caught out. But the judgement of God in Christ crucified is that all of us live under judgement day and daily. There is accountability not in the sense of condemnation or punishment, but in the call to response and to service for the sake of the kingdom. Such is the judgement of the cross. Our ultimate judgement will be the sum of our daily responses to God's loving call to and welcome of us, not least heard and seen in the needs of others: 'Lord, when was it that we saw you hungry and gave you food, or thirsty and gave you drink?' (Matthew 25:37-end).

Jesus the Lamb of God takes away the sin of the world through the judgement of the cross. The shedding of blood frees his sacred life to redeem all life. Just as the High Priest entered once a year into the Holy of Holies to offer in sacrifice the unblemished lamb, and to sprinkle its blood in making atonement, so Jesus the Lamb of God willingly sacrifices his sacred life out of love for us and for our salvation. In the dying there is judgement; paradoxically in the judgement there is new life. The judgement on sin is no sentence on us. Rather, it is an invitation to allow the judgement of the cross to be not our condemnation but our liberation, not our imprisonment but our everlasting freedom.

> Then Christian came to a place where there stood a cross and a little below, a sepulchre. So I saw in my dream that just as Christian came up with the cross, his burden loosed from off his shoulders and fell from off his back and began to tumble and so continue to do, 'till it came to the mouth of the sepulchre, where it fell in and I saw it no more. Then was Christian glad, and said with a merry heart, 'He hath given me rest by his sorrow and life by his death.' (John Bunyan, *The Pilgrim's Progress*)

Prayer
Dearest Lord Jesus, out of love for us
and for our salvation
you endured the agony and the shame of the cross;
help us always to have
in everlasting remembrance
the depth of love
which led you to your tree of glory,
and the weight of sin which nailed you there;
for your tender mercy's sake
we ask it. Amen.

For consideration
How can we speak of God's judgement of the world from the cross?
How can our penal system reflect values of restitution and rehabilitation?
Should there be any place today in our theology for the 'wrath of God'?

The Sacraments of the Cross

By a sacrament I mean the use of material things
as signs and pledges of God's grace
and as a means by which we receive his gifts.
(The Revised Catechism, 39)

One morning, a young boy walked into his grandparents' bedroom and moved across to their bedside table. His grandfather was a bishop, and had left his pectoral cross, the cross a bishop wears, lying there. 'Grand dad', he said, 'Can I ask you a question?' 'Of course you can,' came the reply. The young boy held up the cross and asked 'Is this a key?' Somewhat taken aback by this unusual question straight out of the mouth of 'babes and sucklings', as it were, and with some hesitation, his grandfather replied, 'Yes, I suppose it is.'

The cross is a key, indeed the key into the loving purposes of the God and Father of our Lord Jesus Christ; it is also a key into our understanding of ourselves, of human nature in all its glory and its shame.

I wish to reflect upon the presence of the cross by means of another key; this key is the two dominical sacraments of the church: holy baptism and especially holy communion. Both enable the presence of the cross to be ever present in the church and in the world. In his passion, our Lord made manifest the hidden meaning of his baptism: to service and to suffering. In his passion, our Lord made manifest the hidden meaning of his eucharistic table fellowship: welcome for the kingdom's sake. The values of both are topsy-turvey from an earthly perspective. Before turning to the Eucharist, the institution of which we commemorate particularly each Maundy Thursday, I wish to look at holy baptism by means of another action of our Lord on the same night of his betrayal and arrest which gave his disciples a foretaste of the presence of the cross. This action is recorded uniquely in Saint John's gospel.

We read that after supper, Jesus took a towel, poured water into a basin and began to wash his disciples' feet, exclaiming that 'Unless I wash you, you have no share with me' (John 13:8). The foot washing points to that other sacrament instituted by our Lord which also casts profound light upon the presence of the cross; for this servile action, this foot-washing is a type of baptism. In the early church, the foot washing was associated with the Easter baptismal liturgy in some areas (for example in Augustine's Hippo and Ambrose's Milan). Understood in this way, the foot washing serves not only as an example of humility but also as part of the mystery of our sanctification, our growth in holiness in Christ through the presence of the cross in our midst.

For what is baptism but our cleansing, renewing incorporation into the benefits of our Saviour's passion and death by the gentle yet strong action of the Holy Spirit. Saint Paul speaks of baptism thus: 'Do you not know that all of us who have been baptised into Christ Jesus were baptised into his death? Therefore we have been buried with him by baptism into death, so that, just as Christ was raised from the dead by the glory of the Father, so we too might walk in newness of life' (Romans 6:3-4). Holy baptism therefore becomes the principle of a lifetime rather than the rite of a moment, a constant reminder that our new life in Christ is both gift and graceful response in service of others for the sake of the kingdom. The initiative is our Saviour's and it is eternally linked to his saving passion and death.

Here on the night of his betrayal Jesus serves from

ground level. He would so serve the next day, but from above not below, high and lifted up on the wood of the cross. We can sum it up by saying that in baptism, Jesus serves us by immersing us, washing us in the waters of new life, cleansing us, renewing us in his image for service in his name. The presence of the cross in this and every sacrament is his service to us by, with and through the life of the Holy Spirit nudging us forward, inspiring us inwardly. Well do we pray that 'we may dwell in him and he in us'. Not for nothing is the newly baptised signed with the sign of the cross and in many places the godparents are also handed a lighted candle.

For the sacraments make present and effective in time, here and now, the eternal benefits of our Saviour's incarnate, earthly life: he speaks to us, touches us, cleanses us, feeds us through them. This is part of their many sided splendour – that through the Spirit, Christ still humbles himself for us and for our salvation. They are truly the everlasting pledges of the Lord's abiding love. But if baptism is the sacrament of Christian beginnings then the Eucharist is, *par excellence*, the sacrament of our continuance and growth, to borrow from the sixteenth-century Anglican theologian, Richard Hooker. To its institution we now turn. On the night when he was betrayed, our Lord took bread and wine, gave thanks to the Father, and said, "This is my body, which is given for you – this is my blood. Do this in remembrance of me … This cup that is poured out for you is the new covenant in my blood" (Luke 22:19-20).

Ever since this first 'Do this', Christians have been 'adoing' for century after century. Who can forget these words of the distinguished liturgist, Dom Gregory Dix, surely amongst the most memorable of liturgical prose?

Was ever command so obeyed? Men have found no better thing to do for kings at their crowning or for criminals at the scaffold; for armies in triumph or for a bride and bridegroom in a little country church … On the beach at Dunkirk; for the birth of a child – one could fill many pages with the reasons they have done this, and not tell a hundredth part of them. And best of all, week by week and month by month, on a hundred thousand successive Sundays, faithfully, unfailingly, across all the parishes of Christendom, the pastors have done this just to make the *plebs sancta Dei* – the common people of God. (*The Shape of the Liturgy*, p. 744)

So what are we doing when we do this? At the simplest level we are being our best selves; for once in our lives we are being truly obedient to an explicit command of our Lord. But at a deeper level we are doing something far more: we are proclaiming not only by word but in sacrament the heart of the gospel, which is the three-fold dimension of God's eternal love in Christ for his broken but lovely creation, for you and me. 'Christ has died; Christ is risen; Christ will come again.' Visually, tangibly, sensually, mysteriously, the wholesomeness of the presence of the cross and all its saving benefits are spread before us, mind, body and spirit. Here past, present and future all merge and we are recipients of such glory, for the Eucharist is remembrance, recognition and anticipation all rolled into one feast.

The hymn-writer, William Bright, stresses this three fold dimension of presence when he writes:

We know, when we approach thy board,
That thou thyself art here;
And thus we show thy death,
O Lord, till thou again appear.
(Hymn No. 439)

We remember that this is the memorial of the cross, of our Saviour's passion and death once for all, for us and for our salvation. This is the first dimension, the remembrance of things past – 'Christ has died'.

We recognise also that though we are not bound to the sacrament, Christ is; he is here amongst us. This is the second dimension: the past is also mysteriously present – 'Christ is risen'.

But we anticipate our Lord's return, for did he not say that he 'will never again drink of this fruit of the vine until that day when I drink it new with you in my Father's kingdom'? (Matthew 26:29). Here is the third dimension: the future glory beckons – 'Christ will come again'.

So if that young child whom I mentioned in the beginning were to ask us if the Eucharist is a 'key', we could reply like his grandfather, 'Yes, it is.' It is the key by which the Lord reveals the height and depth of his love for us, the sign of his everlasting service. It is the key by which he unlocks the gate of glory, as we kneel and sacramentally receive him afresh into our broken lives.

We become our best selves not only in the doing, but in the coming and the going, because we approach the table of the Lord, the altar of God, not presuming. 'Nothing in my hands I bring, simply to thy cross I cling.' Our hands are held out, open. To borrow from Saint John Chrysostom, there we make a throne for the Lord wherein we receive in thankful faith this most precious sacrament of our Saviour's abiding presence, so that we may truly 'dwell in him and he in us'.

The Eucharist contains the profound mystery that we do not come to a memorial meal in remembrance of times past. The Lord is *here*, and we are drawn at his invitation to sit and to eat with him that we might be renewed by his welcome to invite others to share this welcome for the sake of and in the service of the kingdom, especially those outside our institutional doors.

In the Eucharist we truly have holy communion. For here, and at every celebration, is proclaimed not only the sacrifice of the cross, but the healing benefits of the Lord of the cross in time and eternity. The Lord Jesus, our great high priest, bids us come that our faltering trust and honest intentions maybe renewed by the power of the cross proclaimed at this and every Eucharist. Well do we sing:

Here O my Lord I see thee face to face;
Here faith can touch and handle things unseen.
Here would I grasp with firmer hand thy grace,
And all my weariness upon thee lean.
(Hymn No. 418)

Prayer
Loving Father, through your gracious invitation
and gentle welcome we are reborn and renewed
in the one breath of the Spirit.
Help us to recognise the signs of your presence
not only in your word and sacraments
but in the needs of others,
especially those outside our churches;
for the sake of your ever welcoming Son,
Jesus Christ our Lord. Amen.

For consideration
What significance does the sacrament of Holy Baptism have for our lives now ?
Has your appreciation of the sacrament of Holy Communion changed much over the years ?
Are the sacraments keys to our understanding of the mystery of God?

The Shame of the Cross

'Looking to Jesus the pioneer and perfecter of our faith,
who for the sake of the joy that was set before him,
endured the cross, disregarding its shame.'
(Hebrews 12:2)

It is the conviction of the Christian that in Christ, God was revealed. The poet John Betjeman expresses it thus:

That God was man in Palestine

And lives today in bread and wine.

(Church Poems: Christmas)

But we do well to note the manner of his 'revelation', born as flesh of our flesh and heartbeat of our heartbeat. As the epistle to the Galatians puts it: 'But when the fullness of time had come, God sent his Son, born of a woman, born under the law' (4:4).

Splendour, light and glory in their traditional forms did not attend the manner of this appearing. God entered into the limitations of time and space, our world, with the cry of a baby. And this cry from within the wood of a manger would be echoed some thirty years later upon the wood of the cross. At his birth, blood and sweat and tears. At his death, more blood, sweat and tears. The blood of his death becomes the blood of our rebirth.

These cries from crib and cross, unite the Lord Jesus with our joyous and saddest moments. This divine conde-scension, this humble identification with the human predicament should stop us in our tracks, and bring us to our knees in wonder. For here is a different insight into our understanding of the meaning of the 'power' of God.

The humility of Jesus, so apparent in his life from cradle to grave, was expressed in unexpected ways through service to, and care for, the outcast and the lonely. I wish to make a connection between this note of divine humility and the events of this week we describe as holy, particularly with the events of Good Friday.

In enduring public arrest and ridicule, in enduring the mocking and the scourging, in enduring the 'shame of the cross' (Hebrews 12:2), our blessed Saviour was dying as he had lived – in humble service to the world God loved, and still loves so much.

But in patiently bearing such shame, our Lord was not only dying in physical agony, but also in public humiliation. In the public eye, there was no more shameful death than crucifixion. Anthropologists of the Greco/Roman world place a heavy emphasis upon the role played in its culture by the code of honour and shame. Society was clearly ordered and regulated. Honour involved status, and shame involved being outside such public respect. This too is involved in the crucifixion of the 'Lord of Glory' (1 Corinthians 2:8). Historical and legal contexts of crucifixion need to be considered, which are these: namely, that to die in such a humiliating way was considered by contemporary society as becoming forever accursed, a public disgrace. To emphasise this point of eternal disgracefulness, victims, in spite of the understandable modesty of artists, were crucified naked. So we read: 'They divided his clothes among themselves by casting lots' (Matthew 27:35).

For a Jew this had a special distastefulness about it as nakedness was considered to be an indecent pagan affectation at the best of times and here, in death, he was being executed by the representative of such practice, Pilate. But worse: citizens of Rome were rarely crucified, because crucifixion was restricted to the colonies as a particularly nasty and exemplary form of punishment to keep, as it were, the natives in check. Jesus endured the shame of being executed by a foreign power according to its laws. It was regarded as fit only for slaves, robbers and terrorists; in short, the lowest types of criminals.

Jesus was therefore numbered amongst them, with the lowest of the low if you like. Hence the significance of him being crucified between two others. Traditionally they have been described as thieves. But the word translated as thief, *lestes*, can also mean a terrorist, someone who opposed by force the Roman occupation of Palestine. Apparently, there were many such bands of terrorists before and after our Lord's time. For example, I recall Josephus, the Jewish historian of the first century AD, recording that on one occasion there were so many crucifixions that there was not enough room around the walls of Jerusalem for all of them.

Recent research seems to suggest that the Romans in Palestine didn't crucify many petty thieves, but they did crucify violent nationalists. So the release of Barabbas the activist has further significance in this light. Jesus quite literally dies in his place – the innocent for the guilty. There is much to ponder here concerning God's redemptive purposes in this and other contexts. But Pilate also uses this particular crucifixion for more strategic purposes – as a means both of asserting his authority to greater effect, by as it were, 'getting at' the Jewish authorities. We read that he had inscribed on the cross in Hebrew, Greek and Latin the title, 'Jesus of Nazareth, the King of the Jews' (John 19:19). Here was the legal justification, that under the *Pax Romana*, there could be no king but Caesar. But this inscription of course was a deep affront to the Jews, and they understandably requested the addition of the words, 'This man said ...' (John 19:21). But Pilate famously replied: 'What I have written I have written' (John 19:22).

It was a scandal to a Jew that anyone claiming to be a king, or a messiah for that matter, would end up on a cross. But what the two rival authorities both failed to see was this: in crucifying Jesus, in rendering to Caesar the things that are Caesar's, Jesus was rendering to the Father the things that are the Father's, namely his life for the redemption, the healing of the world.

So the long and the short of it, or rather the height and the depth of it, is that to the Romans, Jesus was executed for being a king and a rabble rouser. To the Jews, he was but another false messiah amongst many false messiahs who had led some, not least from neglected and under-resourced Galilee, into a false sense of expectation. The best way to be rid of him, especially as Passover quickly approached, was to get the Romans to execute him under their law. However, there is one further shameful twist in this pathetic intrigue. It relates to a Jewish curse which refers to an ancient custom of their hanging executed bodies on trees, again as a means of public example.

The person thus hung was universally recognised as being 'accursed', and the tree known locally as the 'Accursed Tree'. This tradition was taken up by Saint Luke in the Acts of the Apostles, and by writers of early Christian hymns, where the cross is sometimes referred to as the 'tree'. So we read: 'They put him to death by hanging him on a tree' (Acts 10:39). So we sometimes sing: 'Jesus bound upon the tree, fix our wandering thoughts on thee' (*Church Hymnal*, fourth edition, no 101). The emphasis is strongly placed upon the victim being in some way cursed by God. In our Lord's case this is surely the final irony. In spite of Calvary being the city dump of Jerusalem, its most famous tree would transform it into a rediscovered Eden, a new Paradise, through the victory of Christ, 'the second Adam'.

In the light of all of this, no wonder that the apostle Paul in his preaching of the cross could affirm with a deep, but courageous breath: 'But we proclaim Christ crucified, a stumbling-block to Jews and foolishness to Gentiles, but to those who are the called, both Jews and Greeks, Christ the power and Christ the wisdom of God' (1 Corinthians 1:23-24).

To be ashamed is not a pleasant experience either for an individual or for an institution. It is a time for keeping the head down and for keeping out of sight; for saying little or nothing, except perhaps penitently, 'forgive me'. Some-times, we can be ashamed of someone or something to the extent that we become angry or seek to distance ourselves from the event or person involved. The Lord Jesus was not ashamed to endure such emotions. Yet apart from one man, John, it was the women, notably led by his dearest mother, who were willing to partake of humiliation by as-sociation. Intuitively, they knew that each birth was a kind of death and each death a kind of birth. Shame passes. Love alone abides and redeems.

The Lord Jesus takes upon himself in his selfless passion, the shame of the world in all its grubby, selfish sinfulness in order to be true not only to the will of the Father, but to his very self. The pattern of such humility is consummated amidst such shame and degradation. In humility, to the annoyance and surprise of the disciples, he once washed their feet. His blood so serves to wash us eternally from the ravages of sin. In short, our blessed Lord came not so much to die; rather he died as he lived, expending himself, extending himself on the beams of his ever-glorious cross, amongst the battered, broken and bruised of life. Well is it said that 'having loved his own who were in the world, he loved them to the end' (John 13:1). But he still so serves be-cause he still so loves. May we take to heart some words of the writer of the epistle to the Hebrews: 'Looking to Jesus the pioneer and perfecter of our faith, who for the sake of the joy that was set before him endured the cross, disregarding its shame' (Hebrews 12:2).

Prayer
Loving Father, give us courage, great courage
when the forces of wickedness threaten
the goodness and safety of others,
the beauty of your fragile creation,
or when we are falsely accused for your sake.
Enable us to find strength in your nakedness and shame
so to be clothed by your example and fortitude;
for your tender mercy's sake we ask it. Amen.

For consideration
Why is it often so difficult to speak out against injustice or wrongdoing?
Where is the shame of Christ to be found in its liberating power today?
How and where are good people ridiculed today?

The Suffering of the Cross

And about three o'clock Jesus cried with a loud voice,
'Eli, Eli, Lema sabachthani?'
'My God, My God, why have you forsaken me?'
(Matthew 27:46)

No one who takes any interest in the affairs of our planetary home can be in any doubt about the awful weight of suffering borne by so many people in the world today. From the atrocities of war to the ravages of famine, from the spread of disease to the wilful actions of the terrorist, from institutional violence to acts of individual madness. Perhaps tragically, 9/11, September 11th will become a kind of deathly shorthand for all of this, and more. Surely the past century has seen and heard more suffering than any other? Yet, the work, the tireless work of agencies of relief, and of technological and medical research continues at an unrivalled pace in a fellowship of aid, thank God.

Good Friday involves such suffering, such pain and agony; the 'why' of life. It also I pray and trust reveals a remedy, indeed a pledge of eternal worth. At one level, it reflects the age-old problem of why suffering and injustice have to afflict the innocent and the vulnerable. Why one race, one family, one person have to endure so much while others less virtuous sail through life virtually scot free. This eternal dilemma is found throughout the Bible, especially in the book of Job. He cries, 'Why do the wicked live, reach old age and grow mighty in power?' (Job 21:7).

Have we Christians anything to say about this? Have we any comfort, any word of hope to offer amidst the 'encircling, gathering gloom' when confronted by such honest anguish? I think we need to face the fact that in some, perhaps in many dreadful and tragic circumstances, it is far from easy 'to light a candle rather than curse the darkness'. Perhaps in the companionship of the Holy Spirit we do better to remember the example of our blessed Lord, who when pressed for answers in the presence of Pilate, was silent (see John 19:8). Similarly, recalling his sacred example we too can cry out in despair against the dying of the light, 'My God, my God why have you forsaken me?' (Matthew 27:46).

But before we box ourselves into a corner, it is worth remembering that the problem of suffering is, in essence, just as difficult for an atheist to comprehend. Indeed, some of the worst excesses of violence and genocide in the past century have been committed by regimes which were avowedly atheistic. Together, we need to explore ways through this collective ignorance for the good of all. Yet I do believe we Christians can say something about God and suffering by pointing to a 'green hill far away' and to a cross, indeed to three crosses which stand there.

All would admit that the cross is an instrument of the cruellest torture, and when death came, it came dropping, dripping, slowly, breathlessly, primarily through suffocation. But the Christian goes further and looks not upon this means of torture in isolation. Rather, we say, look upon the One who hangs there, upon him 'whom they have pierced' (John 19:37), the Lord Jesus who makes this dreadful scene (and week), amazingly, mysteriously holy.

Look closely; look carefully; see who it is who hangs there. See indeed that 'from his head, his hands, his feet, sorrow and love flow mingled down' (Hymn No. 247). Because of who it is 'who hung and suffered there', we trust that no human experience from birth to death, from the wood of the cradle to the wood of the cross, and indeed beyond, is outside the knowledge and compassion of God.

Jesus has entered into life's darkest, bleakest moment on his cross; the very worst that life can throw at us has been thrown at him, and more: 'He came to what was his own, and his own people did not accept him' (John 1:11). In Christ, suffering is the sacred beat of God's heart of love, for it is in the midst of suffering that our Saviour declares, 'It is finished' (John 19:30). It is in suffering, by his holy and glorious wounds, that our lesser wounds find their home and their healing.

The suffering of the world, the pain and brokenness of our lives, our sense of personal failure and God forsakeness are embraced by Christ's outstretched and pierced arms on the cross, and in union with his suffering, are brought deep into God's heart of healing love. In Christ, in union with the Lord of life and death, whose dazzling body still bears the marks of such passion, suffering can be redemptive; can become the source of a new beginning. The cross says that somehow, someway, suffering can become redemptive. This is very easy to say coming from one who has not, to the best of my knowledge, got a relative suffering from Alzheimer's, Aids or another as yet incurable disease. Easy to say from someone who has not suffered the death of a child, or the death of a relative cut down as a result of a senseless accident or willful act of violence. However in my defence, I am not unacquainted with suffering and with death both at the pastoral and personal levels. Equally, I know that our response to suffering depends often on our temperament: what is major to one individual is minor to another, and vice versa. I know too that the experience of suffering can lead not to new beginnings, but to fresh bitterness and everlasting regretfulness. I know this. But I know also that attempts to remove suffering, its sight, its smell, its touch from the map of human experience is an uncivilised action. Why? Because suffering people can, in many circumstances and 'with sighs too deep for knowing', embrace us, can reach deeply into our condition and minister to us, encouraging us to go on an extra mile journey in their companionship of self discovery, even of renewed love. Further, scripture teaches us that a fruit of suffering is endurance. In the famous *Screwtape Letters*, the Ulster don C. S. Lewis tells the story of letters of advice written by a Senior Devil to one of his subordinates. Here is a piece of it:

> Do not be deceived. Our cause is never more in danger than when a human, no longer understanding but still desiring to do our enemy's [God] will, looks around upon a universe from which every trace of God seems to have vanished, asks why he has been forsaken, yet still obeys God.

In Christ's companionship suffering is where God's loving, self-giving presence is seen in all its terrible beauty, and it is for you and for me to appropriate the measure of its mystery. The body/bread is broken and the blood/wine is poured out at every eucharist for you, for me. Isn't it strange that one of the many symbols of Christ's passion is a snake entwined around a cross? Its origins lie both in the world of the Old Testament and in the Greco/Roman world of the first centuries of the church. For example, Aesculapius, the Roman god of medicine has as his symbol the serpent entwined around a staff, because the serpent was thought to have the power to discover healing herbs, and often it was depicted on their altars as a guardian spirit. Today, it is the symbol for example, of the Royal Army Medical Corps. But the Old Testament background is more apposite for us. Remember Moses, who, when confronted by a plague of serpents in the wilderness, was told by God to take a brazen serpent and to put it on a pole so that all who looked upon it would be healed? Our Lord takes this story and applies it to himself: 'And just as Moses lifted up the serpent in the wilderness, so must the Son of Man be lifted up, that whoever believes in him may have eternal life' (John 3:14).

Perhaps Jesus sensed that when he would be lifted up on the wood of the cross, he would be taking into himself the cruelty, sin and suffering of the world, and through his oblation, his self-offering, would transform them into the source of healing and new beginnings for creation. There is an ambiguity here, for the serpent in Christian theology is seen traditionally as the source of temptation, indeed of evil, in creation. Yet evil itself is part of the healing process. Evil has to be not only confronted and rejected but absorbed and redeemed by the only power which can overcome its sting – the self emptying humility of divine love. As we pray in the words of an ancient prayer, 'O sweet sin, that was found worthy of so great and wonderful redeemer.' In some way the lamb and the serpent are one, are inseparable. Some words from the 25th Discourse of the fifth-century Egyptian Desert Father, Abba Isaiah of Scetis, are helpful here:

> Try hard to fix your eyes on the bronze serpent which Moses made according to God's command. He placed this on the wood at the top of the mountain in order that anyone bitten by a serpent may gaze upon it and immediately recover. Our Lord Jesus on the cross resembled the bronze serpent ... Our Jesus assumed this model in order to extinguish the venom that Adam had eaten from the serpent's mouth and in order to bring back nature – which had become contrary to nature – to conform once again to nature. (from *In the footsteps of the Lord*, Penkett and Chryssavgis, p.22)

Therefore, to those who would obliterate all suffering from our midst and so diminish our capacity for mercy, compassion and discovery, the cross of Christ is a true sign of contradiction. Indeed, our Saviour was not crucified alone, for were there not three crosses on Golgotha? Rather, on the cross, from the cross, he is present, not just alongside, but beside and between the agonised as it were reaching out, stretching beyond, to embrace another in need. And always, as he did to one of the co-crucified, seeking to bring comfort: 'I tell you, today you will be with me in paradise' (Luke 23:43).

In the cross, the agony of God's fragile creation and the agony of God's vulnerable love are inextricably linked and entwined. Under its shadow we must enfold the world's pain in constant intercession to the Father through its High Priest by the tenderness of the Holy Spirit.

I wish to end with a story from another Ulster writer, Helen Waddell. In her memorable book, *Peter Abelard*, we find the hero, Abelard sleeping out under the stars with his friend Thiebault. They hear a cry which rends the night, 'a cry of intolerable anguish', we read. They presume it to be that of a child, but on seeking and finding, discover a trapped rabbit. They quickly release the poor creature from its snare. Abelard says: 'Do you think that there is a God at all? Whatever has come to me I earned, but what did this poor creature do?' Thiebault replies: 'I know.' 'But I think that God is in it too.' replies Abelard. 'Do you mean that it makes him suffer too, the way that it does us?' says Thiebault. Abelard cries, 'Then why doesn't he stop it?' Thiebault responds, 'I do not know. Unless it's like the prodigal son. I suppose the father could have stopped him, but what would have been the use? All this is because of us', he said as he stroked the limp body. 'All the time God suffers more than we do.'

Prayer

Loving Father, help us to understand
that the darkest hour is the hour before dawn;
encourage us to see that with the breaking light
in the gift of a new day,
there is the renewal of hope for those who place their pain
and the anxiety of others in the healing embrace of the
pierced hands of your dear Son, Jesus Christ our Lord.
Amen.

For consideration

How, in the name of God, can any suffering be described
as redemptive?
Does the cross have anything to say in the debate about
euthanasia?
How does the suffering of Christ speak to us about the
compassion of God?

The Authority of the Cross

Take thou authority to preach the Word of God,
and to minister the holy Sacraments in the Congregation.
(from the Ordering of Priests
according to the Book of Common Prayer)

At every ordination of a priest in the Church of Ireland according to the Order of The Book of Common Prayer, the bishop at the moment of ordination says these solemn words:

Receive the Holy Ghost for the office and work of a priest in the church of God committed unto thee by the imposition of our hands. Whose sins thou dost forgive, they are forgiven; whose sins thou dost retain, they are retained.

The power of 'binding and loosing', the authority to pronounce in God's name forgiveness to the penitent, is not the bishop's to give, or the inherent right of an individual person by virtue of their sense of vocation. The authority for such a declaration and for such an awesome responsibility is from the risen Christ, our great High Priest, and is delegated by him through the Holy Spirit to the church in the ministry of its priests. It is uniquely focused in what we are reflecting upon each Good Friday; it speaks *'urbi et orbi'* about the authority of the cross in time and for eternity. For it is through the sacrificial death of Christ in complete self-giving love that the sorrowing, penitent sinner, you and me, finds new life, new motivation, fresh springs for adoration and for service. Truly we assert with Saint John:

For God so loved the world that he gave his only Son, so that everyone who believes in him may not perish but may have eternal life (John 3:16).

It is the very goodness and holiness of God revealed in Christ crucified that leads us to repentance and to accepting into the fibre of our being that forever precious fruit of his passion and death, and that 'pearl of great price', the forgiveness of our sins. Here too is no compulsion, here is no worldly authority. We are to find rest for our souls in its gentle shadow.

We grieve for our sin not out of fear of God; we grieve for our sin not out of doubt of his abundant mercy; we grieve for our sin not out of fear of hell. We grieve for our human weakness and frailty because it has wounded God's heart of love, because our sin and the collective sin of society to which we all contribute and in which we all share, has nailed the Lamb of God to the tree of shame.

We certainly do not presume to come before such cup-overflowing love trusting in any personal merit or individual status, head held high as it were. Rather are we driven to our knees before the mystery of it all. We are brought low when the realisation of our part in such scenes of cruelty seeps into our consciousness. Well do we sing: 'Nothing in my hand I bring, Simply to thy cross I cling' (Hymn No. 557).

The authority of the cross is the authority of divine forgiveness in Christ, and it is the life blood and *raison d'être* of the church, that one institution which exists for the sake of those who are as yet not at home or welcome within it. Such a gift is offered so that each one of us may mature into our best selves in the companionship of Jesus in the family of his body the church. Such authority runs counter to the authority of the world which usually pertains to order and to control – not necessarily bad aims in themselves, but they can stifle individuality and initiative, and when confused with power, they can be diabolical in their exercise.

The authority of the cross serves to remind us that ultimate authority is subject to the judgement and mercy of Christ and him crucified, and that in communion with the Holy Spirit, the bond and bearer of such love, we are personally and collectively to seek out the values of the kingdom for the welfare of all. At the heart of such a task lies the call to repentance and to forgiveness. It is in this rhythm of sorrow and new beginnings that the heart beat of the world is renewed and restored.

The Christian life is rooted and grounded in the soil of Calvary: that is, in the call to receive and to offer forgiveness, the authority of the cross. The use to which we put this divine medicine, this precious balm for the world weary is vital, for by it the world recognises the sincerity of our commitment to Christ and our appreciation of the cost of our healing. This also runs directly opposite to all secular humanistic views of life which omit any reference to the divine, and seek to assert that as we are the measure of all things, we can make and remake ourselves better. Or if we acknowledge the existence of a God at all, it is only out of deference to one or two facts, pieces of a jigsaw as yet undiscovered – the God of the few remaining gaps if you like.

But this is not the New Testament's understanding of creation or of human nature. Certainly our goodness is affirmed in the beginning, and creation's diversity and incompleteness is recognised. Yet, our 'brokenness' too is never far from focus: 'How often should I forgive? As many as seven times?' (Matthew 18: 21). Indeed did not the One who hangs before us from his cross of glory once say: 'For I have come to call not the righteous but sinners' (Matthew 9: 13)? In other words, those who recognise their need not only for God but for his cleansing love to restore and to renew. But the authority of the cross goes further and declares that we have no right, no authority of ourselves to presume on our capacity to forgive. Well do we say, 'To err is human and to forgive is divine'

Yet we know in the depths of our being that when we refuse to offer forgiveness, we are less than human. Equally, when it is withheld from us we feel trapped and burdened by guilt. We cannot escape from the two-edged sword of our recognition of the priority of forgiveness to oil the relationships of life, and that to be a forgiving person we need to know the power of forgiveness in our own life. For the church, and by implication for the world, such forgiveness is fundamental to the day of days we call Good Friday.

The church which is formed out of forgiveness for forgiveness, has the propensity to turn its back on such a *raison d'être*, be it in its dealings with the marginalised within and without its broad bounds, or people of other faiths or none. The list is endless. Just think of those who believe that they have been hurt or injured by you or by me. There is something odd, to say the very least, about the churches urging reconciliation in the world without taking to heart the incongruity of such a plea in the context of its own divisions and restlessness.

Theories abound as to how Christ's death assures us of God's forgiveness. These are not really competing 'christianities' but are explanations of this wonderful truth that far from appeasing an angry God, Christ's sacrifice was the complete and all-sufficient expression of the love of God for his lovely but broken creation. His heart is our hearth. So we hear again these encouraging, life giving words:

But now in Christ Jesus, you who were once far off have been brought near in the blood of Christ. For he is our peace (Ephesians 2: 13-14).

Prayer

Loving Father, help us not to doubt your love of us;
help us not to hide our need and weakness from you.
Rather, by the grace of the cross may we turn to Christ
and experience in the Holy Spirit
his forgiveness and love which alone can set us free
to become our best selves in the service of the kingdom.
This we ask through Christ our Lord. Amen.

For consideration

Do you experience the public confession of sin in the liturgy as liberating ?

How scandalous to the call to forgiveness is 'christian' disunity?

Share any experience of freedom or liberation you have experienced, and see if they relate in any way to the cross of Christ.

Mary and the Cross

'How can this be, since I am a virgin?'
(Luke 1:34)

Did Mary have any choice? you may well ask. Well, she certainly had a question: 'How can this be?' What a question! We too have our questions, significant and apparently less so, when confronted by life's choices, its agonies and its joys – the 'changes and chances of this fleeting world', hows, whys, whens and wherefores. Questions seek answers, and hard questions seek profound answers which often, wisely in the event, remain unanswered, at least this side of judgement. Mary received her answer though – a divine one, as mysterious and ultimately as difficult as her question. Yet she appears to accept it by faith, on trust. The rest you could say is 'salvation history'; but it also becomes my history, your history, our history here and now.

I ponder often if she could have said 'No', and sometimes after a hard day in the parish if she *should* have said 'No!' I believe that she could have said 'No', bearing in mind what we have already considered. I cannot imagine our life 'in Christ' not allowing for the possibility of a 'No'. Indeed, wouldn't it be blasphemous to say the opposite?

You may think my use, once again, of blasphemous a bit strong; but which is the greater blasphemy: to say that God who created us lovable and free would create one equally lovely but unfree, or, to allow for the possibility that she whom the Liturgy of Saint Basil describes as the 'Joy of all creation' could have said 'No'? If in Christ God is no respecter of persons, he is at the very least a defender of our integrity and dignity, of our liberty. Therefore, the possibility if not the likelihood of a 'No' is real. Then what – no incarnation? God being God, 'that which nothing greater can be conceived', would have found if not a better way then another way, wouldn't he? But would he? I'm not so sure. The manner of his coming 'in Christ' reveals one fact only: he seeks our cooperation, nay participation. It tells us of no 'plan B' in the event of a breakdown in negotiations. For from Mary's 'yes', all heaven and indeed hell breaks forth: and Simeon said to Mary: 'A sword will pierce your own soul too' (Luke 2:35).

Mary's choice, her 'yes' reveals to us, in a less spectacular context of course, just how embracive our choosing of God's choice of us can be, mind, body and spirit; and this we discern in the ensuing dialogue with the angel, the heavenly messenger. Mary's question, her 'How can this be?' (Luke 1:34) speaks of the mind, of reason's reasonable response to the greeting 'Hail Mary'. But such questioning must go deeper and further – into the depths of the heart. The answer came: 'The Holy Spirit will come upon you' (Luke 1:35), which speaks of reason's limitations and takes us deeper into the realms of wonder and awe. It speaks of matters too deep for reason alone; it points to the soul/ heart, and much heart-felt 'pondering' resulted.

But even mind and heart are not sufficient in enabling our choosing. There is a calling forth of a total commitment of personality, of body/will as well. 'You will conceive in your womb and bear a son' (Luke 1:31). This speaks not just of mind and heart but of the body's active, indeed painful participation in the mystery of the divine revelation. It speaks of our becoming places where the Holy Spirit abides:

For none can guess its grace
Till we become the place

Wherein the Holy Spirit
makes his dwelling. (Hymn No. 294).

No Holy Spirit, no Christ within. This entire dialogue, the
hem of which we have barely touched, enforces the truth
that 'matter matters to God', by speaking of a death to self
and a leap of faith into God's trustful purposes for us 'in
Christ'. (This mind, heart, body rhythm is mirrored in cer-
tain devotional practices of prayer and scripture reading,
notably those of Saint Sulpice and of *Lectio Divina*.)

No wonder that, thirty-three or so years later from these
Annunciation mysteries, Jesus by candle light speaks to
the reasonable Nicodemus thus: 'No one can see the kingdom of God without being born from above' (John 3:3).
Nicodemus is naturally mystified and questions further;
but again Jesus asserts the initiative of the Holy Spirit:
'The wind blows where it chooses ... so it is of every one
who is born of the Spirit' (John 3:8). The fruit of such pene-
trating dialogue is hardly mentioned again by John,
(Nicodemus disappears 'off stage' if you wish.) However,
we meet him again in the company of Joseph of
Aramathea, asking Pilate for the body of Jesus for burial.
Soon the tomb will become the womb of the new creation,
our new life 'in Christ'. Later, Saint Paul will affirm: 'If the
Spirit of him who raised Jesus from the dead dwells in
you, he who raised Christ from the dead will give life to
your mortal bodies also through his Spirit which dwells in
you' (Romans 8:11).

Mary's 'yes' involves the totality of her being. Her choice
is the key to the door of salvation history, for the hopes and
fears of eternal as well as temporal years held their breaths
awaiting the response. Her 'yes' pointed both to joy and to
sorrow for her, contentment and pain, pleasure and misun-
derstanding, laughter and the heavy drops of grief. But also

for us. Her 'yes' reveals a pattern of friendship which begins not with our faltering faith in God, but in his loving vulnerability to pass amongst us unrecognised, even unto death. This may speak to the delicate and oblique as well as to the hostile within and more probably without our sadly separate 'households of faith'. Renewed emphasis on such 'holy communion' could replace the usual polemics between the churches concerning Mary's place in the Communion of Saints, and draw us ever closer to the import of her words at Cana: 'Do whatever he tells you' (John 2:5).

Mary is Mary, you are you and I am me; each of us is different from her, and from one another. Yet the same Spirit which beckoned her beckons also to us. If the implications of the beckoning are somewhat different, the call is as definite. There are parts of our being, at least from my experience, where the Holy Spirit gains little access. Mary would surely urge us to go the extra mile and allow baptismal grace to be liberated by the refreshing presence of the Holy Spirit, gentle yet powerful. For 'in Christ', each of us has been called to be a bearer of the life of the Spirit. But as Mary soon discovered, the Holy Spirit is 'cross shaped' as well as 'dove like'. Death to self is never far away. Mary's 'yes' reveals the earthiness of such faith, and that discipleship begins in the soil, the humus of our lives, day by day, as the Holy Spirit seeks a dwelling place where his fruit of 'love, joy, gentleness, peace...' can spring forth (See Galatians 5:22f). Ours is a welcoming, non presumptive Lord, who seeks to 'pick us up and to dust us off', to take us step by step in faith, hope and love along the path of eternal life by the Holy Spirit, making all things new, longing to welcome us by his beckoning, welcoming 'seeking our hesitant 'yes'.

Indeed, Saint Paul writing to the church in Corinth boldly asserts:

For the Son of God, Jesus Christ, whom we proclaimed among you, Silvanus and Timothy and I, was not 'Yes and No'; but in him it is always 'Yes'. For in him every one of God's promises is a 'Yes' (2 Corinthians 1:19-20)

Prayer
Loving Father, your call to each of us in Christ
is made in love.
Help us to be more attentive
to the opportunities of response
through all of life's many demands
and in the turning back to you
to rediscover our image restored and renewed,
for the sake of our Saviour Jesus Christ. Amen.

For consideration
Is it true to say 'no Holy Spirit, no Christ within'?
What is the importance of Mary for ecumenical dialogue?
How does the pattern of Mary's 'yes' find an echo in our lives?

The Cross and Advent

And the city has no need of sun or moon to shine on it,
for the glory of God is its light,
and its lamp is the Lamb
(Rev 21:23)

I greatly enjoy the Advent season, primarily because of its mood. On the one hand, it has a smokey, fireside feel about it. On the other, it contrasts in the one breath light and darkness, works and grace, mortality and immortality. The music too is sombre from its hymnody to its great chorales and concluding O Antiphons which, if you are fortunate, are often sung in the setting of impressive and moving liturgy. Its liturgical 'colour' is violet amidst sparse sanctuaries, serving to remind us that Advent is a season of anticipation and preparation, but not as the world understands it. It is a season of penitent anticipation and preparation. It is a solemn reminder, amidst the money-making, of weightier matters than the anticipation of party invitations, or the preparation of Christmas card and gift lists. In as much as they are expressive of the joy which beckons in the celebration of the birth of Christ, well and good. But we should note, however, that it is a celebration which traditionally should last for 12 days, commencing with our Christmas communion, which must be focused upon and gathered around the great and mighty wonder of the incarnation. We need annually, don't we, at least 12 days to take it all in? Advent always brings to my mind some words of the late Archbishop Michael Ramsey: 'The first hope of every Christian is the hope of heaven: the first, the nearest, the most relevant of his hopes. Does that surprise you?' (A. M. Ramsey, *Freedom, Faith and the Future*, p.41)

Not when we understand that Advent encourages us to lift our hearts and minds above the trimmings on the table and wrappings under our feet, from things temporal to things eternal – to the dawning of that which is yet to be, heralded by and in the birth of the world's Redeemer. The hope of which the archbishop speaks embraces the totality of the life of the incarnate Lord and not only the birth: his passion, death, resurrection and ascension. Advent must help us to prepare in heart and mind for all of this and more, because the embrace of his incarnation is, like his robe, seamless, without ending or beginning. The Christmas 'eucharist' gathers all of this of course, and depending on the church calendar used in your parish, the wisdom of the tradition draws this out by following Christmas Day with the feasts of Saint Stephen and The Holy Innocents. Where Christ is, death as well as life is at hand, indeed is at stake for the pilgrim.

In the past, Advent was a time for preaching about and reflecting upon the 4 Last Things: heaven and hell, death and judgement. We should recover our nerve and readdress them. Apart from the first, what is hopeful about the rest, we may well ask? Well, the hope is first and foremost God's hope alongside and within us in Christ; God's hope for his wounded yet redeemed creation. Our responding hope is that in Christ, the kingdom has dawned and that the prophetic hopes and fears of all the are fulfilled in him. That there will indeed be a 'realisation' of a ' heaven and a new earth', the fruit as much of the 'torn curtain' (Mk 15:38) as the broken waters, for the Lamb of sacrifice is at the 'centre' of all (see Rev 21:1ff). It is in the shadow of the cross as much as in the shade of the stable that Christ is born and must be reborn by grace in us. In short, it speaks of the eschatological dimension of all things in Christ, of times and seasons, about which at the same time, no one knows, yet towards which we all must journey inexorably (see 1 Thessalonians 5:1ff).

The Collect of Advent used in the Anglican tradition throughout the season, composed by Archbishop Thomas Cranmer, beautifully captures both the mood and rhythm of the season:

> Almighty God, give us grace to cast away the works of darkness and put on the 'armour' of light, now in the time of this mortal life in which your son Jesus Christ came to visit us in great humility; so that, on the last day, when he shall come again in his glorious majesty to judge both the living and the dead, we may rise to the life immortal, through him who lives and reigns with you and the Holy Spirit, now and ever. Amen

The dominant contrasts within the collect are those between light and darkness, mortality and immortality, time and eternity. Advent serves to remind us that we all live *sub specie aeternae*, that is, under the umbrella of eternity. In Christ, eternity has broken into our world of dates, hours and fixed points of reference. The doxology says it all:

> Glory be to the Father and to the Son and to the Holy Spirit; as it was in the beginning, is now and ever shall be, world without end. Amen.

The glory has dawned in Christ, a glory without end. But as Saint John reveals, such glory is supremely revealed on the cross:

> I glorified you on earth by finishing the work that you gave me to do. So now, Father, glorify me in your own presence with the glory that I had in your presence before the world existed (John 17:4-5).

Ramsey comments: 'The cross is the event of glory, by it there is the revelation of eternal glory and from it there comes the mission of the disciples, their consecration in the truth, their sharing in the unity of the Father and the Son and their coming to the glory in heaven' (M. Ramsey, *Be still and know*, p 48).

Advent cautions us, in the words of another beautiful collect, to 'so pass through things temporal that we finally lose not the things eternal' (Trinity 4). It urges us to so do by reminding us of beginnings and endings, of birth and death and judgement. Of a specific birth to be precise. That of our Lord Jesus Christ. But our life and the offer of eternal life through the life of this holy child is brought before us at this season. In his beginning is our end, for the church teaches that the Babe is also the world's Redeemer.

Beginnings are so important in life. We don't need a sociologist, a child therapist or even a priest to tell us so. Common sense dictates such an appreciation. Advent prepares us for not just the beginning of the Christian story, but for those who travel deeper, our stories too, for it brings all heaven before our eyes. It points to endings by reminding us of our tender beginnings in Christ: our baptism, our confirmation, our first holy communion, our first intimation of the holiness and majesty of God. What are such moments for? Mere ends in themselves or points of departure on a lifetime's journey to be converted into a pilgrimage of faith, hope and love in the fellowship of the Holy Spirit? A pilgrimage whose ultimate destination is heaven. Ponder long about such beginnings, auspicious or inauspicious. See how they are enfolded in the mantle of love that surrounds the child in the manger. See how the door is ever open to welcome other travellers from nearby hills to distant deserts. Be awake to the breaking in and the breaking open of God's time in our circumstances, individual and collective. Attentiveness is all.

Prayer

Heavenly Father, in the birth of your Son
you consecrate all time to your eternal purpose of love
by the Holy Spirit.
Enable us so to travel that we lose not
the vision of your holiness
nor become insensitive to your presence
in the needs of your creation;
so that, at the last, you may complete in us
what you have by grace begun;
we ask this through Christ our Lord. Amen.

For consideration

How true is the comment that our first hope is the hope of heaven?

How is the cross linked to Advent?

How can we escape the rush of Christmas in the season of Advent?

The Cross and Christmas

This will be a sign for you:
you will find a child wrapped in band of cloth
and lying in a manger.
(Luke 2:12)

In the midst of many gifts at this most holy festival, we gather year by year to give thanks for the greatest gift of all: the gift of God's loving, abiding presence in Jesus Christ. Well do we assert: 'For God so loved the world that he gave his only Son' (John 3:16).

He gave not a passing splendour, nor a bright yet waning star. We Christians believe that he gave us his Son. More, we believe that he gave us his very life that 'everyone who believes in him may not perish but may have eternal life' (John 3:16). Well do we bow in profoundest gratitude with 'angels and archangels', with Saint Joseph and the Blessed Virgin Mary, with the shepherds and the magi, before this 'great and mighty wonder'.

This gift of gifts comes to us wrapped not in paper and tinsel, but incarnate in a life, a very tiny life. And this life is itself wrapped not in ostentatious wealth but in rather inauspicious circumstances, summed up by all that the traditional crib scene symbolises. The tiny baby is supported both by the presence of his parents, and the wood of the manger-crib. And this 'double presence', these two life-supports of 'parents' can help us as we seek to understand how we can open up this eternal gift of the love of God in Christ for each one of us, as we continue our pilgrimage in this third millennium of his most sacred birth.

First, the parents. It is by, with and through the loving obedience of both Mary and Joseph that this momentous event in their lives, and ultimately in the life of the cosmos has come to pass. Yet theirs is no unswerving obedience. Rather, their part is the part of questioning faithfulness, hinted at by Mary's fearfulness: 'How can this be?' (Luke 1:34), and Joseph's social embarrassment expressed in his: 'dismiss her quietly' (Matthew 1: 19), on learning of her pregnancy prior to marriage.

Yet in all this human confusion the Holy Spirit rested, inspiring trustful togetherness: both are told on separate occasions, 'Do not be afraid' (Matthew 1:20; Luke 1:30).

As a consequence, they set out for Bethlehem from Nazareth in response to a directive from Caesar Augustus during the governorship of Quirinius. We read in timeless prose: 'And she gave birth to her first-born son and wrapped him in bands of cloth, and laid him in a manger, because there was no place for them in the inn' (Luke 2:7).

I often keep company with Joseph and Mary. Fearful of God's loving purpose in my life and questioning my faithfulness; yet I still journey on, ever 'nudged on' by the Holy Spirit, no matter how I may despair about the quality of my discipleship.

Take comfort from Joseph and Mary then in 'keeping on keeping on'; for slowly but surely, the Holy Spirit is at work in our lives bringing to birth the light of Christ within, which is a real fruit of the Holy Spirit, 'guiding our paths as may best for us be'. Be aware of the presence of questioning faithfulness in your pilgrimage. Neglect not the prayer to the Holy Spirit when overtaken by a spirit of fearfulness. Doubt and faith are comfortable bedfellows when honestly expressed and set within the context of worship. Indeed the opposite of faith is not doubt as is commonly believed. The angel did not say 'doubt not' but 'fear not' to fearful Mary.

The other 'support' from the Nativity scene, alongside the example of Joseph and Mary, is the manger, or more specifically, the wood of the manger. Just as the heavenly star reflects the light of the Christ child, and so illuminates our understanding of the baby's significance in terms of light and cosmic universality, so too the wood of the manger resonates with mystic meaning. It prepares us for the wood of the cross. The meaning of Christmas Day is only 'seen backwards' by Good Friday, Easter and Pentecost for the church. We only celebrate Christmas because of Easter. The babe is to become our Saviour. Saint John in his gospel explains: 'Indeed, God did not send the Son into the world to condemn the world, but in order that the world might be saved through him' (John 3:17). More, the telling of his birth links this birth into time and space expressed through the history of a people peculiarly expectant yet strangely unprepared for 'such a coming'.

Note again the emphasis on the banishment of fear. Jesus has come not for condemnation but for deliverance. A Christianity or a church which primarily inculcates fear and condemnation is not worthy of the name, or of the worship of our Lord Jesus Christ. Because God has revealed the fullness of his love, not his condemnation, in the life of the one whose mysterious birth we celebrate every Christmas. And this 'amazing love' is seen in all its terrible but glorious beauty from the wood of the cross. The wood of Calvary's tree and the wood of Bethlehem's manger are cut as it were from the same timber, are engrained with the same patterns of divine love which seeks both to uphold and to enfold our faithful fearfulness all our days. The baby is the son of the carpenter and Son of God in the one breath. The meaning of his life is the loving purpose of God in our life and the life of the cosmos 'unto salvation'. Both the wood of the manger and the wood of the cross affirm this to the 'ages of ages', and in every millennium.

I was given this little poem by an old priest friend many

years ago, and have treasured it ever since, without knowing its authorship. It is a mini commentary on the incomparable prologue of Saint John's gospel which is traditionally read on the Feast of the Nativity, Christmas Day. It seems to me that it also points forward in several respects to Good Friday, and binds together the loving purposes of God revealed in both the nativity and the death of our Lord Jesus Christ in terms of light, peace, and love. I end with its deceptively simple words:

Light looked down and beheld darkness;
Thither will I go said Light.
Peace looked down and beheld war;
Thither will I go said Peace.
Love looked down and beheld hatred;
Thither will I go said Love.
So came Light and gave sight;
So came Peace and gave rest;
So came Love and gave healing;
AND THE WORD BECAME FLESH
AND DWELT AMONG US,
FULL OF GRACE AND TRUTH (John 1:14).

Prayer

O Lord Jesus Christ, before whose sacred crib and sacred cross we bow and kneel in adoration, grant us never to part from your gentleness nor to refuse your forgiveness, but so to be transformed by both that we may be a blessing to others; for your tender mercy's sake we pray. Amen.

For consideration

Is it correct to say that we can only understand Christmas in the light of Calvary?
Is the expression a 'faithful fearfulness' not a contradiction in terms for a Christian?
Should the church expect special treatment of the observance of both Christmas Day and Good Friday?

The Cross and Easter

After these things
Jesus showed himself again to the disciples
by the Sea of Tiberias.
(John 21:1)

We note that it is early in the morning and not at night when the Lord appears to the disciples for the third time as recorded by Saint John. It is by a lakeside and not on a road. It is in the heart of familiar Galilee and not the more anonymous Emmaus. However, as at Emmaus, we do not recognise the person. Unlike Emmaus, it is the sound of a voice and possibly the gait of the speaker, not the action of a supper time meal which releases the senses of recognition.

I remember speaking to a friend who was a keen, a very keen and experienced angler, a freshwater fisherman to be precise. In the course of our opening remarks which quite naturally focused upon the beautiful weather which we were enjoying at the time, I said it must be lovely weather for fishing. I couldn't have been further from the truth. 'No!' he quickly replied. 'Why?' I asked. 'It's too bright,' he replied, 'The fish can see you a mile off. You need darker, danker weather if you are going to have any luck.' So there you have it – too much light and warmth was not to my angler friend's liking. This short conversation not only enlightened my ignorance, but gave me an insight into our Lord's resurrection appearance to the disciples by the lakeside in Galilee.

The disciples fished not in the daytime but we read at night, probably for the same reason. Further, they knew pretty well every inch of the lake we know as the Sea of

Tiberias. They knew its numerous little harbours and inlets which blended into its broad and wide shoreline, as well as its depths and shadows. It is a very open lake indeed, but presumably even at night the darkness 'is no darkness' to the experienced eye of the Galilean fisherman. It is, from years of family lore and experience, an ideal cover for them. Indeed, I recall reading somewhere of reports which indicated how some fishermen would set out in their boat with only the light of a blazing torch to aid their sight as they stood gazing into the sea until fish were sighted and, quick as lightening, they would fling their nets into the water. However, often in the morning, they return empty netted, down hearted and very tired. I also recall another story of two men going out to fish. One wading waist high in the water with a net, the other on the shore. The 'shoreman' acts as a sort of watchman as he has a clearer view and can shout to the 'waderman' to throw his net in to right or to left. His visibility, though directly removed from the arena of action, is in fact better than that of his friend who is right in the middle of the scene. The gently sloping shoreline provides both a good vantage point and its still background a perfect sounding box.

In our story there is a strange combination of these two anecdotes, for there is both a weariness from fishing unsuccessfully and there is also a 'shoreman'. But there the similarity ends, for on hearing the voice in the dawning hours, the disciple fishermen respond as if for one last time, in hopeful desperation of a catch: 'Cast the net to the right side of the boat and you will find some' (John 21: 6).

Here, in a strange sort of way, is a new annunciation for they are being encouraged to become bearers, heralds of the dawning kingdom. Like Mary, they could have ignored the invitation. But the Lord knew where and how to find them and Oh, why not? In a sense, their obedient response is not unusual. Anything was worth a last ditch effort after such a disappointing night's work, especially as they were almost to shore; one last 'fling of the net', as it were. But, of course, the voice from the gloaming, the stranger on the shore, is no ordinary 'shoreman'. John recognises this. Soon, Peter jumps out of the boat crashing from the last supper to the first breakfast. Jesus says to them: 'Come and have breakfast' (John 21: 12). It is all there amongst the pebbles and the rocks. William Blake comes to my mind:

> To see a world in a grain of sand,
> And heaven in a wild flower,
> Hold infinity in the palm of your hand,
> And eternity in an hour.
> (*Auguries of Innocence*, 1)

Saint John now adds: 'This was now the third time Jesus appeared to his disciples after he was raised from the dead' (John 21:14). In the village of Emmaus, we were in a scene of despondent domesticity. However, our Lord, un-recognised on the way, was recognised in the taking, breaking, blessing and giving of bread (see Luke 24:13f). Action spoke louder than words. It was as we have said, evening.

But here, morning has broken, the chill in the air over-come by the warmth of the fire, and the unsurpassed mys-tery of the presence of their Risen Lord. Christ is known primarily not in an action shimmering with 'eucharistic' intimations, but in a call, in a way, re-commissioning and ultimately to renewal. But in both, revelation is an en-counter through the pain and toil of disappointment. In spite of the similarity between the two stories, not least their sense of intimacy (dare I say even a sense of divine playfulness?) and continuity with the past – a meal in a vil-lage house; amongst the disciples by the Sea of Galilee

where it all began three or so years ago – there are important differences.

I hope I am not over stretching things if I say that if
Emmaus has a 'churchy', institutional feel to it, this story has
a 'worldy' ring to it. In Emmaus, word and sacrament meet:

> Were not our hearts burning within us while he was
> talking to us on the road, while he was opening up the
> scriptures to us ... they told what had happened on the
> road, and how he had been made known to them in the
> breaking of the bread (Luke 24:32 and 35).

How true in this context is an understanding of the church
as a building which exists for the sake of the breaking open
of the word and the celebration of the sacraments.

But God forbid that the Lord is Lord only of the church,
limited by restriction to a place for particular liturgical
functions, vital as they are to our growth in grace. The
lakeside story from Saint John reminds us that God's loving presence is for the world, for it resonates both with
echoes of the past and hope for the future – with call and
mission: Christ choosing the fisherman, Christ calming a
storm, Christ feeding and preaching to crowds of people,
Christ resting in nearby hills, Christ healing in nearby vil-
lages, not least in Capernaum. In short, the Lord is back in
the familiar, amongst the nine-to-five life and people of his
beloved Galilee and region. He knew where to find his
friends, and so returns home as it were to bring them, and
through them, us, home to him. But for a purpose: 'To live
out the wonderful works of him who has called us out of
darkness into his marvellous light: the truth about Jesus
Christ, the same yesterday, today and forever; and in so
doing, to enable many others to make the surprised, aston-
ished and joyful discovery that Christ is risen.' (*Signs of
Hope*, David Hope, pp. 163-4)

But he comes at dawn to make the old ways fresh and new, to make the possible real, to encourage them once again to leave behind the familiar, leave behind their boats and come fishing anew with him. We note that he did not order them to stop fishing, to leave their nets immediately and follow him. He encouraged them to fish in the right place and direction. There is no condemnation, only the confirmation of personal worth and of their labour. But life could not be the same for them. Their 'new life' rediscovered in their 'old ways' would begin afresh with this dawn of the church's missionary call.

But even here the life, the liberating life of the cross is revealed. Affirmation is all. Does not the charcoal fire recall for Peter the last time he sat at fire close by Jesus, and denied him thrice before dawn? Now this fire of the dawn would by its very smell and sound, never mind its symbolic offering of bread and fish, cauterise away the wounds of the night fire of 'Galicantu', the open wounds of his denial, of his rejection, of indeed his tears. As if to confront Peter with this awful memory in order to heal him, our blessed Lord, possibly sensing Peter's embarrassment and shame, draws him aside quietly after breakfast and asks him three times, 'Do you love me more than these?' (John 21:15).

In so doing, Jesus stirs up afresh the flame of Peter's desire to follow Jesus as the embers of the breakfast fire grow dim: 'Lord, you know that I love you' (John 21:16).

Truly, as the poet has written, 'The fire and the rose are one.'

The dove descending breaks the air
With flame of incandescent terror
Of which the tongues declare
The one discharge from sin and error.
The only hope, or else despair

Lies in the choice of pyre or pyre –
To be redeemed from fire by fire'
(T. S. Eliot, Four Quartets: *Little Gidding*)

Prayer
Dearest Lord, your sacred body still bears the marks
of your passion and death.
Open our eyes to the signs of your Risen presence
in the morning, at noon and at evening
not least in the familiar places of our lives
and the lives of those whom we love;
for you are our Way, and Truth and Life.
For your love's sake we ask this. Amen.

Questions
How easy is it for us to recognise the risen presence of
Jesus in the 'familar' circumstances of life?
How can our past be confronted and healed by Christ?
How central is the resurrection to the life of the church ?

The Cross and Pentecost

*To them God chose to make known how great among the
Gentiles are the riches of the glory of this mystery,
which is Christ in you, the hope of glory.
(Colossians 1:27)*

Personal testimony to the love of God in the life of the be-
liever has a vital and overwhelming biblical basis to its
place in the corpus of tradition. Equally, anyone who is
familiar with the corpus of tradition, never mind the scrip-
tures, knows this to be true. What about a Paul or dare one
mention Augustine? Yet, for most of us in many quarters
there is an understandable reluctance to share in this way
for a variety of justifiable reasons, amongst which must
rank large feelings of unworthiness and possibly embarrassment – embarrassment not only for the teller, but for
their listener too.

Yet in speaking of the Cross and the Holy Spirit in the
one breath, there must be a degree of personal integrity
about so telling. Because it is the Holy Spirit who liberates,
indeed mediates the innumerable benefits and graces of
the Saviour's passion and death, the victory of Good
Friday and Easter for the church and the world, into and
through the life of the penitent pilgrim disciple. If this be
the case then there must be at least a hint of first hand ac-
quaintanceship with such a glorious mystery.

Therefore, speaking personally and with no little reti-
cence at this point, I can say that I first became truly aware
of the relationship between the Holy Spirit and the cross
when I attended (with other students for the sacred ministry from the Church of Ireland Theological College) the
first Church of Ireland Renewal Conference held in Dublin
in 1980 convened by the late Archbishop John Armstrong

of Armagh, the year before my ordination as deacon in the church of God. There is no need here to go into the circumstances of the Conference save to say that I was aware of a degree of aridity in my spiritual life at the time, and of the need for refreshment. I was of course theologically attuned to the importance of such a remedy lying with the work of the Holy Spirit in the life of the Christian, but was extremely wary, due to previous unconvincing encounters, with the Scylla of biblical fundamentalism and Charybdis of charismatic enthusiasm. How to steer a safe course between these two dangers from my perspective, without of course seeming to 'quench' the Holy Spirit in any way, was a prerogative. The talks and worship were certainly helpful, and the waters seemed relatively calm. The night before the Conference closed, I decided to ask a clerical couple with whom I came into conversation to pray with me, which they kindly did without any immediate obvious 'charismatic' effect, thank God!

During the course of the final day I found myself taking particular notice of a text, which was only fleetingly referred to by a speaker: 'If the Spirit of him who raised Jesus from the dead dwells in you, he who raised Christ from the dead will give life to your mortal bodies also through his spirit who dwells in you' (Romans 8: 11).

Why this text above all others? I have no idea why it stuck in my consciousness. But I do know that during the closing worship I experienced what I can only describe as a profound sense of peace and joy which seemed to permeate my whole being, accompanied by a gentle tearfulness. This emotional feeling was strengthened by a realisation of the love of the crucified Lord for me through the mystery of the resurrection. In short, Christ is alive by the Holy Spirit to the glory of the Father. Why that text from Romans became for me the key, I don't pretend to know. Enough said.

Please forgive this testimony to the reality of the touch of the Holy Spirit in my life (not least any friend who truly knows me and for whom this may all appear too much to take – come off it Barrett!). But please accept it as a statement of a vital stage in my pilgrimage which, although I have failed abysmally to express it in all its joyful fulness in the course of my priestly peregrinations, nevertheless 'made the connection' for me between the work of Christ crucified and risen, and the role of the Holy Spirit in the life of the pilgrim disciple today and everyday.

The life of the Holy Spirit dwelling deep in and bonding the mystery of the Holy Trinity bursts forth in the beginning in creation, and through the Easter mysteries in our re-creation, conveying to us the merits of the victory of bloodied cross and empty tomb. For the Holy Spirit is the unity and diversity of the love of the Father and the love of the Risen Son in the church for the sake of the kingdom: the *koinonia* of the Trinity. What the passage from Romans revealed and keeps on revealing to me is of course no new thing – that Jesus did not raise himself. Rather he was raised in the power of the Holy Spirit to the glory of the Father. But that such life, such love seeks us out so that he may indeed abide in us by grace. Well do we sing:

O Comforter, draw near,
Within my heart appear,
And kindle it,
They holy flame bestowing.
(Hymn No. 294).

Jesus says: 'Because I live, you also will live' (John 14:19). This can also be translated: 'Because I live on, you too shall have life', and elsewhere in John's magisterial gospel account, the Lord affirms: 'I came that they may have life, and have it abundantly' (John 10:10) It is all gift; all of the

Holy Spirit who makes effective here and now to the faltering yet hopeful pilgrim the riches of the mystery of Good
Friday/Holy Saturday/Easter Day: the Easter Triduum.

What of Easter Eve, of Holy Saturday? This most neglected of Holy Days (in the Church of Ireland at least)
seems to say to us that it is as much in our awareness of the
absence of the 'Lord and Giver of life', as in our sensitivity
to the new life, that the Holy Spirit is at work. All times are
in his hands and all circumstances. For even in death, even
here love abides: 'He was put to death in the flesh, but
made alive in the spirit, in which also he went and made a
proclamation to the spirits in prison' (1 Peter 3:18-19). In
the darkness, indeed in the helplessness at times of faith,
the Holy Spirit is at work: 'The darkness is no darkness
with you but the night is as clear as the day: the darkness
and the light are both alike' (Psalm 139:11).

Holy Saturday seems in itself to involve both death and
life, and so outlines for us the pattern of Christian discipleship which is, a death to self to find self in the companionship of Jesus, by, with and through the gift of the life of the
Holy Spirit within us. This most extraordinary of days has
a strong pentecostal character about it. It is a kind of liturgical expression in the church's calendar of part, a small
part, of the meaning of baptism. It is not without significance that the early church saw fit to baptise its catechu-
mens on the evening of this day, and in so doing, to proclaim the power of the love of God in the death and resurrection of Christ as Saint Paul teaches in Romans 6:3-4: 'Do
you not know that all of us who have been baptised into
Christ Jesus have been baptised into his death, so that, just
as Christ was raised from the dead by the glory of the
Father, so we too might walk in newness of life?'

The font has been described as both the 'tomb and the
womb of faith' because of the new life in Christ being im-

parted by the Holy Spirit to the candidate through his/her identification with both the death and resurrection of Jesus 'in the waters'.

There is a 'Love Divine' which excels all other loves, a joy which the world cannot take away, a peace which passes all understanding. It is the work of the Holy Spirit to reveal such mysteries to us, and it is the work of a lifetime. Each one of us, particularly if we are ordained, needs to pray for a deeper experience of the Holy Spirit in our lives, not for self's sake, but for the sake of the cross of Christ in the service of the kingdom. If by the life of the Holy Spirit we can confront part of the darkness and fear within by incarnating the light of the Holy Spirit deeper within (as Saint Paul outlines both in Galatians 5:16-26), then we will become more gentle and more courageous Christians in the process. But it is, believe me, a path with many a twist and indeed a sting in its tail. I close with these memorable words of the late Greek Orthodox Metropolitan Ignatius of Latakia, spoken to the World Council of Churches General Assembly in Uppsala, Sweden in 1968. In matters pertaining to the Holy Spirit, it is wise to let the Orthodox have the last word, and none could be more impressive than these:

> Without the Holy Spirit God is far away, Christ stays in the past, the church is simply an organisation, authority is a matter of propaganda, the liturgy is no more than an evolution, Christian loving a slave morality. But in the Holy Spirit, the cosmos is resurrected and grows with the birth pangs of the kingdom; the Risen Christ is there; the gospel is the power of life; the church shows forth the life of the Trinity; authority is a liberating science; mission is Pentecost; the liturgy is both renewal and anticipation; human action is deified.'

Amen to this; the best is yet to be.

Prayer
Holy Spirit of creation,
Holy Spirit of the new creation,
Through the life, death, resurrection
and ascension of Christ,
Come and fill us with your beauty and gentleness,
Your strength and truth,
That we may witness to the reality
of Christ's healing love
to the glory of the Father. Amen.

For consideration
What is our understanding of the Holy Spirit in our lives?
What has the charismatic tradition of the past thirty years
to say to the institutional churches?
How do we neglect the Holy Spirit as Christians?

The Cross and the Holy Trinity

The grace of the Lord Jesus Christ,
the love of God, and the communion of the Holy Spirit
be with all of you.
(2 Corinthians 13:13)

It is usual in Anglican circles to begin a sermon with a prayer to the Holy Trinity, such as this one: 'In the name of the Father, and of the Son and of the Holy Spirit. Amen.'

'Why?' you may ask. Because in so doing each of us, and not just the preacher, is publicly acknowledging that all that we try to do in and through the life of the church, is done in the name of and to the glory of God Father, Son and Holy Spirit. For our brothers and sisters long since departed this was no unusual thing; rather, it was commonplace in the Celtic realms. Actions and activities, be they great or small, were never undertaken without a recognition of the presence and protection of the Holy Trinity. From rising to sleeping, from kindling a fire to milking a cow, all were undertaken in the context of asking a blessing of God the Holy Trinity. Take for example this short prayer:

The Father, the Son and the Holy Spirit,

may the three in one be with us day and night.

Or again:

May the three help my wishing,

may the three help my willing,

may the three help my walking,

and my knees without weakening.

But perhaps the best known of such prayers is St Patrick's Breastplate, where the writer uses thoughts and words which echo the sixth chapter of St Paul's Letter to the Ephesians and seeks to 'Bind unto myself the strong name of the Trinity, by invocation of the same, the three in one and one in three' (Hymn No. 322) for protection and for strength in times of trial or danger.

Thankfully, such a hope is not restricted to the past. Recently, I blessed a newly-wed couple in the name of the Holy Trinity; recently, a baby was baptised in the name of the Holy Trinity. Recently, a sick patient was anointed in the name of the Father, and the Son and the Holy Spirit. The Holy Trinity is as close to us as our breathing in such contexts, of beginnings, middlings, and endings. Indeed, as we leave each act of worship we go forth under the blessing of the Holy Trinity.

In seeking the blessing of the Trinity we are proclaiming the kernel of our faith, which is that God is love, and that such love is uniquely expressed and experienced as a unity in diversity: a three in one and one in three. There is if you like a diversity of persons – the Father, the Son and the Holy Spirit. Yet equally, there is a unity by, with and through love: the love of the Father, the love of the Son, the love of the Holy Spirit. God bound in one eternal community fellowship of love. Such divine love bursts forth in different yet harmoniously loving expressions: in creation, supremely that of the Father in the beginning; in re-creation, supremely that of the Son in his redeeming work; in renewal, supremely that of the Holy Spirit, the 'Lord and Giver of life'. Yet, all is held in a unity: the seamless robe of loving purposefulness. The community of love which is at the heart of Father, Son and Holy Spirit bursts forth in creation, recreation and renewal.

Those who have 'tasted and seen that the Lord is good' (Psalm 34:8) have entered into the very beauty of God. Creation, recreation, renewal are three gloriously liberating and loving activities of the Father, the Son and the Holy Spirit. By such we know that we are held and upheld in and through love, supremely revealed in the cross. For it is in the life, death and resurrection of the Lord Jesus that the mystery of this Trinitarian love is made flesh of our flesh and heartbeat of our heartbeat. For it is at the Lord's baptism that the Father's words are uttered: 'You are my Son, the Beloved' (Mark 1:11), and it is here too that the Spirit descends 'like a dove' (Mark 1:10).

This cup-overflowing, this new life-creating love, finds its earthly home in Christ Jesus our Lord, and reveals its abundantly 'recreative' nature by showing that there is no restriction, no barrier to the access of such love save human willfulness and selfishness. This the wood of the crib and the wood of the cross affirm. Neither does such love in Christ compel anyone to love in return. There is always the waiting, welcoming love of God in Christ. We are free to come and are often, alas for our sakes, free to go. Too often, we take the road too well travelled. We do well to recall these wise words of Denis the Areopagite: 'The Trinity is present to all things, though not all things are present to it.'

In the other reflections I endeavour to outline the context and content of the cross, and its relationship to us on 'high and holy occasions'. I hope also that such contemplation may indeed bring us to our senses by bringing us to our knees in penitent wonder. It is only within the liberating embrace of the cross that such a perspective can truly trace the pain and the glory which beckons. Truly we are on 'holy ground' here, for we are dealing with not only the mystery of the love of God but also the mystery of what it means to be truly human. It is intimately related to the life and the love of the Trinity for truly as has been well said: 'There was a cross in the heart of God before there was one planted on the green hill outside Jerusalem.' (D. M. Baillie, *God was in Christ*, p 194). But the cross of the Lord and above all, the Lord of the cross, affirms world without end, this wonderful life-affirming, heaven-confirming state-ment of the Greek Father of the second century, Saint Irenaeus of Lyons, that: 'The glory of God is the living man; and the life of man is the vision of God.'

In the Spirit, through the Son, to the glory of the Father: that is the movement of faith and of love. We seek to enter into this mystery that the loving mystery may more fully enter us, so that we all may become liberated and liberat-ing people, not for our sakes, not even for the sake of the church, but for the sake of the kingdom of God. Thank God that 'New every morning is the love' (Hymn No. 59): the love of the Father, the love of the Son, the love of the Holy Spirit, three in one, making and remaking our yester-days by the embrace of forgiveness, and calling us to new possibilities by restoring our dignity in Christ. Well do we bind unto ourselves the strong name of the Trinity, Father, Son and Holy Spirit, each and every day.